There is talent out there. Good talent. Talent you desperately want to hire but, guess what? They are (a) hiding from you, (b) do not have their resume posted online and / or (c) are rarely open to new opportunities.

So, how do you reach people like that? You get them to come to you. How? With content. That's what this book is about.

Content is the new sourcing.
by: Jim Stroud

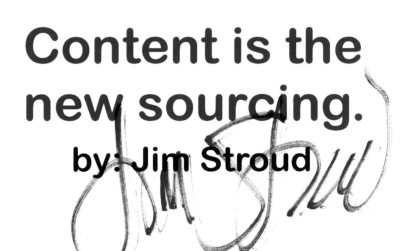

Content is the new sourcing.

By: Jim Stroud

A very big thank you to those who bought my first book and to every owner of this new one. I appreciate you more than you know.

For that matter, big love to everyone and anyone who said to me "good job," or shared one of my videos, or listened to one of my podcasts, commented on a photo I took, laughed at one of my corny jokes, retweeted me, gave something I said a "plus one" or a Facebook "like." I heard you. I appreciate what you did. Thank you for encouraging me.

And last, but certainly not least, thanks to my wife who supports me in her own way. Any achievements I have amassed are due in part to her support. :-)

-Jim Stroud

So, why write "Content Is The New Sourcing?" Well, the purpose of my last book - "**Resume Forensics**" was to teach you how to find passive candidates on the internet. My intent was to keep it short and sweet and in retrospect, I may have made it too pithy. Thus, the book you have in hand now.

JUST A HEADS UP

The verbiage and tone is meant to be conversational and not academic. In reading this, I want you to feel as if we just met in a Starbucks somewhere and by chance became engrossed in sharing sourcing strategies with one another. With that in mind, on to the next paragraph!

In all modesty, the need for this book (and others like it), will increase over the next few years and reso-nate for decades. Why? In a word... millennial. If you are in HR, then you are well acquainted with the word. Its the name of the latest generational work-force; those people born between Queen's "Bohemian Rhapsody" (1976) and Alicia Keys' debut album - Songs in A Minor (2001).

According to the US Census Bureau [1], the Millen-nial generation (aka "Generation Y") will comprise half of the workforce by 2018. Even more significant than their sheer numbers, is the cultural values they bring with them. For example, unlike the "Baby Boomers" (those who preceded Gen Y two generations prior), they do not expect to work one place until they retire. Quite the contrary, millennials tend to switch jobs within the first three years. [2]

[1] US Bureau of the Census, Projections based on 2000 Census

As such, retention is sure to be a MAJOR issue for companies for the foreseeable future. But, that is not what this book is about. (Hmm... maybe the next one will be?)

The next best thing to keeping the people you have is having a pipeline of talent on tap to pull from when the need arises. And that is something I can help you with. ;-)

RECRUITING AIN'T EASY

What comes as no surprise to experienced HR professionals is the fact that recruiting ain't easy. No matter how bad an economy might be and despite the proliferation of applications that flood a recruiter's inbox when a job is posted, the "right fit" is often elusive. Moreover, getting a hiring manager to move quickly on a candidate can be a lesson in frustration for the recruiter as well. The most daunting of obstacles however is the inconvenient truth that some of the more talented people out there, simply do not want to be found by recruiters. I suppose for some, recruiters are a necessary evil at best and at worst, relentless telemarketers who refuse "no" as an answer.

ITS NOT ME MR/MS RECRUITER, ITS YOU

I read a lot, or rather, I try to. Some of what I read really resonates and never leaves me. Such is the case with a certain blog post [3] written by Joel Spolsky the CEO of StackExchange, a growing

[2] The Cost of Millennial Retention Study | http://bit.ly/19aHnRm

network of 111 question and answer sites on diverse topics. I really thought what he said about finding great software developers was spot on. Here is a quote to ruminate on.

> The great software developers, indeed, the best people in every field, are quite simply *never on the market.* The average great software developer will apply for, total, *maybe,* four jobs in their entire career.

> The great college graduates get pulled into an internship by a professor with a connection to industry, then they get early offers from that company and never bother applying for any other jobs. If they leave that company, it's often to go to a startup with a friend, or to follow a great boss to another company, or because they decided they really want to work on, say, Eclipse, because Eclipse is cool, so they look for an Eclipse job at BEA or IBM and then of course they get it because they're brilliant.

> If you're *lucky*, if you're *really lucky*, they show up on the open job market once, when, say, their spouse decides to accept a medical internship in Anchorage and they actually send their resume out to what they think are the few places they'd like to work at in Anchorage.

> But for the most part, great developers... they get to work wherever they want, so they honestly don't send out a lot of resumes or apply for a lot of jobs.

[3] Finding Great Developers | http://bit.ly/9zM2Jl
[4] What It's Like to be Recruited | http://bit.ly/kjlfly

Another blog post along the lines of what Spolsky opined is from CodeBrief [4] and gives the perspective of the highly sought after talent. It did not reflect well on the recruiting profession. A few quotes for your review:

> Roughly three months ago (in the beginning of March), for a variety of reasons, I decided to put my resume out there on the interwebs. Here I chronicle my experience being a software developer on some of the most popular and widely used job channels...

> As I write this, all in all I have received: **266 emails** and **96 voicemails**. This roughly equates to 12.7 emails and 4.3 voicemails *per workday*...

> I also wonder if companies realize that many of their candidates are acquired through pseudo-spam...

> I predict that in the coming years the demand for top talent will be even higher and companies will need to resort to new ways to find and incentivize developers...

Are you familiar with Google Suggest? When you search Google for, whatever, Google gives you suggestions based on the search history of its users. Look what happens when you begin searching "recruiters are…"

recruiters are

recruiters are **idiots**

recruiters are **liars**

recruiters are **parasites**

recruiters are **stupid**

Press Enter to search.

DON'T CALL US! WE'LL CALL YOU (...OR TEXT)

So, how do you reach people that do not advertise their skills, do not want to be found by recruiters and / or have a disdain for recruiters in general? In a word... content.

What is content?

Content is information and experiences that provide value for an audience.

CONTENT IS THE NEW SOURCING

As a rule, your content must be irresistible to your audience. It should be entertaining or informative or (for lack of a better word) "shareworthy." In fact, it is critical to the survival of your enterprise for a number of reasons, most notably, for the purposes of search engine optimization (SEO).

For the uninitiated, search engine optimization is the process of maximizing the number of visitors to a particular website by ensuring that the site appears high on the list of results returned by a search engine. One way to boost your chances of rising high in the search engines is to have strong social signals pointing to your content. Social signals are Facebook likes, Tweets, pins on Pinterest, comments, etc. In other words, the more people tweet, comment, give a Google Plus One, et cetera, to your content, the more your content is validated in the eyes of search engines and rewarded with a higher ranking.

> "We know that social signals are increasing in importance with regard to Google's ranking algorithm, and will continue to do so."
> - Jayson DeMers on SEOMoz.com [5]

In the world of search engine marketers, this has been a very hot topic. So much so, I am beginning to see services appear that propose to increase your search engine ranking by getting more likes, tweets, plus ones, et cetera, for your website. Check out SocialSignifier.com as an example of this.

By the way, check out this chart from Searchmetrics [6] citing Google Search Ranking Factors in the US. Seven of the top ten factors are social signals! [7]

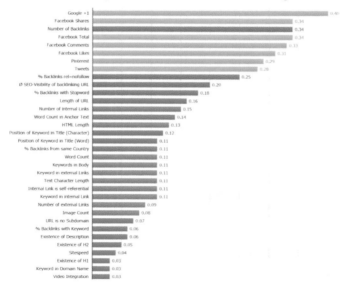

[5] SEOMoz is an industry leader in the field of search engine optimization.
[6] Searchmetrics produces digital marketing software and services.
[7] Want a closer look at the chart? Go to: http://buff.ly/193yEi5

This is great for recruiting!

Not only is there a SEO advantage for having remarkable content that is shared, liked, et cetera, but you are also getting exposed to the social network of those validating your content. This is easy to see! If say, Jacob, tweets an article I wrote on my blog, then everyone who is following Jacob on Twitter has the potential of seeing my content. These are people I might not have been reaching through my efforts alone. Make sense?

Hmm... Let me go off on a tangent here. (I won't be long. Promise.)

TANGENT BEGNS HERE

It's a good thing to repost some of your content at different times of the day so as to maximize expo-sure. People who may see the tweet you posted at 9:30am EST are not necessarily the same audience who sees your tweets posted at 6:00 pm EST. Make sense? Such being the case, I would suggest experimenting a bit with titles and times for the same bit of content. For example...

8:00 am - I love Wednesdays. Getting it done!
2:00 pm - Hump day baby! Say it with me!
7:30 pm - Wednesdays are the best! Do you agree?

I would do this on Twitter (for sure), but also on those social networks where I am very active with my updating (LinkedIn, Instagram, Google Plus, et cetera). However, if I do not post a lot on... umm... say, my Facebook page, then I would space these reposts a lot further out. For example...

January 3rd - What do you think of my cubicle? I decorated it myself. [Pictures of my cubicle attached.]

January 24th - I challenged my fellow cube dwellers to a cubicle contest. I think mine is decorated best. Give me a like if you agree. [Pictures of my cubicle attached as well as cubicles of my co-workers.]

See what I did there? I repurposed the content I posted before and did not share exactly the same information as before, although they are similar. (wink)

OKAY, MY TANGENT IS OVER NOW

Recognizing the importance of social signals now, I would strongly suggest that you add links to your company's social media presence wherever possible. I am thinking of places like in your email signature, business card, company website, marketing collateral and so on. Make sense?

But wait a sec'...

This is bad for recruiting!

How can this be bad for recruiting? If your content is not compelling and only consists of generic job descriptions and sanitized corporate language, no one is going to tweet that, like it or comment on it. As such, your website will sink in the search engine rankings and eventually into obscurity. (Gasp! Maybe even page two in a search result or worse.) [8]

If your company does not invest in increasing social signals, you will pay the price of being invisible on search engines. And the only way to increase those signals is to have content that is GOOD. (Make sense?) Now, let me give you something else to worry about.

Your content should not only be good enough to keep your company out of search engine obscurity, you have to get as many people as possible to connect with your site. Why? Personalization.

In an effort to give you the best search results possible, search engines take into account various factors. In the case of Google, things that are considered when you search include: your location, your past search history, websites you have given a "plus one" too and the activities of your Google Plus contacts and other things I am not privy too.

This is why when you do a search for "platform" you see information about "computing platforms" whereas your friend in London sees data about "Platform" an activist website. (See the difference for yourself! Search Google for something, then do the

[8] Page 1 results get 92 percent of all traffic from the average search, with traffic dropping off by 95 percent for Page 2. According to Search Engine Watch: http://buff.ly/1eZUYug

same search on Google.co.uk)

So, take this scenario into account. Let's say I visit your website and glance it over and leave. I then go to your competitor's website and give it a plus one. And for argument's sake, let us say that you both are in the business of producing steel. A week or so later, I do a search on metallurgy and because I gave your competitor a plus one, their website appears higher in my search results than yours. Why? Personalization. I gave your competitor a plus one and that signaled to Google that said website is more valuable to me personally than another website (yours) because I did not validate it with a plus one or anything else.

Does this mean that I do not see your website at all? Nope, not saying that at all. I am simply saying that I see your competitor's website first and maybe, **maybe**, I see yours later. Its also possible that your website is now on page two and I do not see it at all. But who knows and what has that cost you? Maybe a hire. Get me?

Wait. Its getter better, depending on your view point. Someone I am connected to via Google Plus, say Carmen, is doing a search on metallurgy. Since we are connected on Google Plus and I gave your competitor's website a plus one, your competitor will now appear higher in her search results. Why? (Say it with me.) Personalization. Google figures that if Carmen's friends like a site, then she may have an interest in it as well. And who knows? Maybe my plus one knocked your site to the second page.

Is this causing you some concern yet? I hope so.

Okay, something else to think about. I told you that content is critical to your company's online presence due to SEO considerations and personalization issues. But, you know what? Those things are measurable and can be analyzed. (For example, how many followers and likes you have gained over time or, visitors from a website.) But what about those circumstances that are beyond your reach? I am speaking of the "dark web."

The "Dark Web" is the part of the internet that is not indexed by search engines. And for the clueless, that is a lot more that is not indexed verses what is. I am resisting the urge to go into another tangent and possibly lose you so, let me share some examples of dark web data not indexed by search engines.

- Content shared between people via instant messenger (Skype, Whatsapp, GTalk, etc.)
- Content shared via secret Facebook groups
- Content shared via email
- Content shared via mobile apps
- Content shared via private LinkedIn groups
- Content shared on private Google Hangouts
- Databases accessible by subscription (Monster, CareerBuilder, et cetera)

If you are privy to the analytics of your career website and wanted to know where your traffic is coming from, the dark web is not represented and that could be a significant percentage. However, how can you know? For that matter, Google is not making it any easier by encrypting all keyword searches. [9] In

[9] Read: Google to Encrypt ALL Keyword Searches: Say Goodbye to Keyword Data http://buff.ly/18lzOVB

doing so, you will not be able to see what search engine queries lead to your website.

STARTING TO MAKE SENSE?

I can get really geeky about this stuff, just in case you did not notice that before. The point of this is to stress how important it is to have great content. Most of the results you will be able to track, some of it you will not but the more it is shared, the better it is for your recruiting efforts. Okay, I am taking a breath now before going on to something else.

SO, WHAT IS "GOOD" CONTENT?

Good content is information that resonates with your audience. ('nuff said) To insure resonance, know who you are talking to and say it in a language they can understand. The strategy to achieve that is wrapped up in personas.

Do you know what a persona is? Personas are fictional characters created to represent different user types that might use a site, brand or product in a similar way. Consider the type of person who would have an interest in the billboard shown below.

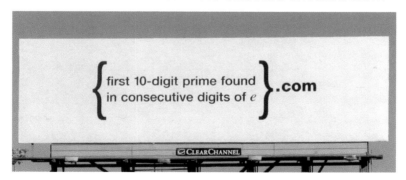

The billboard speaks to the curious in general. There is no clear indication of whom the sponsor is nor of an advertising message. Specifically, it speaks to math students and/or scientists who cannot resist a good puzzle. Some have been known to spend hours trying to figure it out. Whomever is successful at solving the riddle, Google (the company behind the billboard), would love to hire them. Not only because of their numerical prowess but because, they are "geeky" enough to not let an unanswered math question go unaddressed. [10] Such mindsets would be a fit in the Google culture.

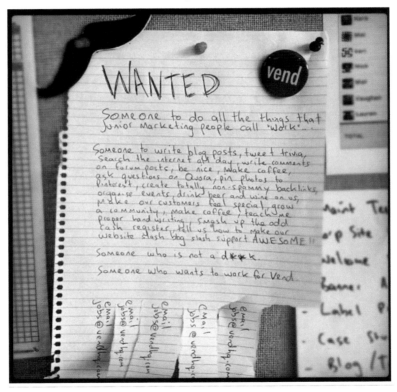

[10] Read: Google Entices Job-Searchers with Math Puzzle : NPR http://buff.ly/198ngBy

Vend is a cloud based point of sale software company that is (at this writing) looking for "junior marketing people" that are skilled in social media, creative and fits into the culture of the company by not being a "d**k."[11] Obviously, their culture includes people who are not offended by the implied language. The person Vend is targeting is also a bit playful, which is what the fake moustache in the upper left corner suggests to me. I also think the person they want is someone in college, with little professional experience. The requirement of making coffee and spiral notebook paper seems to speak to that, at least to me.

The U.S. Military has been using video games for some time to attract recruits. [12] Why? Video games encourage and develop decision making skills and strategic thinking in a variety of environments. Just the sort of skills crucial to survival for the soldier on the ground. Someone who can excel in these types

[11] Read: 5 Ways to Attract Candidates http://buff.ly/1giewgy and Have you met Vend? http://buff.ly/1detkl5
[12] Read: How the American military is using videogames to capture the hearts and minds of children http://buff.ly/1dexa3O

of video games (and meet other military requirements) would be of interest to a military recruiter.

DIFFERENT STROKES FOR DIFFERENT FOLKS

As you can (hopefully) see, different strategies are
needed for different recruitment needs. An army
video game would not attract insurance actuaries nor
would a mathematical puzzle on a billboard speak to
a political cartoonist. In each case, the personas that
best fit those campaigns are vastly different. All
things being considered, a question of how to build a
persona remains.

There are a lot of methods and strategies one could
use to build a persona. I'm going to share the means
I would use to build one. However, I would
encourage you to so some research on "how to
create a persona." It can't hurt. (smile)

HOW TO CREATE A PERSONA
(FILL IN THE BLANKS)

WHO ARE THEY PROFESSIONALLY?

- I want to attract ___(insert job title here)_____.
- The talent I want is an expert in _____.
- In the past, she or he has probably accomplished
  things like _____.
- They most likely want to work on a project that
  involves _____.
- The talent I want is different from others in his /
  her position in that they _____.
- The talent I want would most likely ask me
  questions about _____.
- Job titles they had in the past include _____.

WHERE ARE THEY FROM PROFESSIONALLY?

- The talent I want most likely worked for such companies as _____.
- The talent I want probably graduated from such schools as _____.
- The talent I want probably attends conferences like _____.
- The talent I want probably talks online about _____.
- The talent I want would have worked with such luminaries as _____.
- The talent I want lives in _____ or at least, is open to relocation. If that is not an issue, then the talent I want has worked virtually for _____ many years.

WHAT DO THEY WANT PROFESSIONALLY?

- The talent I want to hire would be interested in our company's _____.
- The reason why the talent I recruit wants to work for us verses a competitor is _____.
- The talent I want to hire would have concerns about _____.
- The talent I want to recruit is probably used to a compensation package of _____.

WHO ARE THEY PERSONALLY?

- The talent I want is motivated by_____.
- The talent I want has a goal of becoming a _____.
- The talent I want tends to be an extrovert or an introvert? They are an _____.
- Does the talent I want work alone or in a team?

Once you have the answer to those questions, add them to a form akin to the one below. Of course, change my gobbledegook to actual information that you can use. If you can get it all on one page, then great! If not, flip over and add more data on the back.

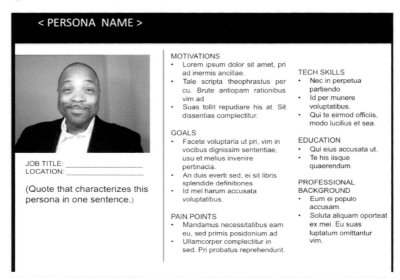

I would also suggest that you share the personas you build with employees already serving in that role, those who work alongside them and the hiring managers they will be reporting to. Said coworkers could serve as a type of focus group and ideally, validate your theories. When meeting with them, bring the following items and discuss them ad nauseum:

- **Sample Resumes** - Do the resumes presented in your meeting fit the overall needs of the requirement? Are they in line with the persona created?
- **Projects** - Discuss project overviews currently in the works and in the past. How do they fit in the daily work life of your personas?

- **Selling points** - What can honestly be said to present the company in the best light possible?
- **Refusal Points** - What are the dealbreakers that would potentially halt a hire? Is there anything that cannot be compromised?
- **Interview questions** - What would be questions that would help identify candidates as an outstanding cultural fit?

KNOW YOUR ENEMY / KNOW YOURSELF

I would use the feedback from your focus group to tweak the persona you created, but I would do a SWOT analysis of my major competitors before making it "official." Um... you know what I mean by SWOT, right? SWOT is an acronym for strengths, weaknesses, opportunities and threats.

Recruiting is war. Knowing what your rivals will be pitching to your potential hires is just as valuable as knowing what you have to offer. All things being equal, it could be the edge you need to wrestle that star candidate away from everyone else. (wink) To do a SWOT analysis, simply answer the following questions.

STRENGTHS

- What stands out about the competitor?
- What types of benefits do they offer?
- How are they on work-life balance?
- What is their measure of growth per year?
- What is their reputation and rank in the industry?
- How long has the organization been in operation?
- Do they have a specialty or niche that appeals to candidates we're trying to recruit?

WEAKNESSES

- Where are their locations? Do candidates want to work there?
- How does the company portray itself?
- What do the employees say about the company?
- Any rumors of layoffs?
- Which jobs have been posted the longest and presumably, hardest for them to fill?

OPPORTUNITIES

- Are your benefits comparable or better than your rivals?
- What do you offer that your competition does not?
- What type of advancement opportunities are they offering to the type of candidates you are recruiting?

THREATS

- What is your competitors forecasted growth?
- Is your competitor in expansion mode?
- Was your competitor recently featured in the media?

Some of the data you find will be public information (press releases, job postings, executive interviews, et cetera), other data may be gleaned from conversations (interviews, discussions with alumni from competitor companies) and the rest may simply be speculative. However, the more you are able to discover information like this, the better off your personas will be. Make sense? Hope so.

QUICK RECAP

Sometimes I ramble, or at least, I feel that I am. For the sake of my own paranoia, let me do a quick recap of what I've been trying to say.

- Recruiting is challenging.
- Some of the people you want to hire do not want to be found by you.
- You need good content to attract the attention of passive candidates.
- Good content is information that resonates with the audience you want to recruit.
- To make "good" content, you need to know who you are trying to attract. Personas are key for that.
- You need to know your competitors and what they are offering so you can out maneuver them when competing for star candidates.

SHARE IT, DEVELOP IT, MAKE SURE IT GETS SEEN

When it comes to content as a recruiting strategy, be sure to follow one simple rule: Share the good stuff, develop even better stuff and make sure that your stuff gets seen by your intended audience. Here are some tips on how to do all of those things or at least, tip the scales in your favor.

HOW TO FIND CONTENT THAT IS WORTH SHARING

One way to find content worth sharing is to find blog posts discussing a certain topic which have a large number of comments. Logic being, said blog post is resonating with that audience else they would not be responding so much. Make sense?

Check out this blog search I did on Google.

"50..200 comments" site:wordpress.com "space tourism"

And below are some of the page one results.

space tourism | Space Cynics (yep, we're back!)
spacecynic.wordpress.com/category/**space-tourism**/ ▾
Posts about **space tourism** written by shubber, Thomas Olson, ... the alt.space community because the era of **space tourism** was finally here. ..... **75 comments**

For the Record | Wayne Hale's Blog
waynehale.wordpress.com/2013/06/02/for-the-record/ ▾
Jun 2, 2013 - ... for earth imagery, a commercial market for satellite communications, probably a commercial market for **space tourism**. .... With **97 comments**

THE TRUTH BEHIND THE SCENES | ACTUAL AND REVEALING ...
thetruthbehindthescenes.wordpress.com/ ▾
May 18, 2012 - Posted on May 15, 2012 | **62 Comments** .... flights and space activities, including **space tourism** and space commercialization, increase.

Do you get what I did there? If not, let me break it down bit by bit.

"50..200 comments"

In this part of the search I am using Google's numrange command to find online websites that have the phrase 50 comments OR 51 comments OR 52 comments on up to 200 comments.

site:wordpress.com

Here I am asking Google to not search the entire internet but instead, focus on web pages that are on the domain wordpress.com. (Wordpress.com is a very popular blogging platform.)

"space tourism"

I am asking Google to find me web pages that have the phrase "space tourism" on it.

If you do a double take on the results shown on the previous page, you'll see where the first result is a blog post with 75 comments, the second has 97 comments and the third has 62 comments.

As I mentioned earlier, Wordpress is a popular blogging platform. However, it is not the only game in town. Other platforms you may want to search are:

- Livejournal.com
- Blogger.com
- Squarespace.com
- Typepad.com
- Blog.com
- Weebly.com
- Edublogs.org

Another Google search for finding popular blog content is the following:

inurl:"tag/linux" security "20..500 comments"

Article Series on Linux Device Drivers - LINUX For You
www.linuxforu.com/**tag/linux**-device-drivers-series/ ▾
10+ items - Series. Device Drivers · Lisp Programming · Apache **Security** ...
May 3, 2012   9 Comments   Device Drivers, Part 17: Module Interactions.
February 28, 2012   27 Comments   Device Drivers, Part 15: Disk on RAM ...

Linux Distros For The Paranoid: What Are The Most **Secure** Distros?
www.makeuseof.com/**tag/linux**-distros-paranoid-**secure**-distros-si/ ▾
by Danny Stieben - in 124 Google+ circles
If you're a Linux user, **security** was probably one of the benefits that made you switch from ... By Danny Stieben on 2nd July, 2012 | Linux | **51 Comments**.

Tag: Linux | Citrix Blogs
blogs.citrix.com/**tag/linux**/ ▾
... type of virtual desktop - each specifically tailored to meet the performance, **security** and flexibility . ... By Ray Yang · Published on 5 years ago · **35 Comments**.

For the sake of clarity, this is the logic behind my search.

inurl:"tag/linux"

I am asking Google to search the URL of websites for the phrase "tag/linux".

security

I am looking for webpages that also have the word "security" cited on them.

"20..500 comments"

As you may have guessed from the last example, seeking blog posts with as few as 20 comments and as many as 500.

Blogs are generally "tagged" which is why I do not
have my search restricted to a blogging platform like
wordpress. (Tagging is when a blogger categorizes a
blog post.) Oh! There may be times when you want
to know what blog posts have been recently getting a
lot of comments. You can do that by refining your
results to a certain time period. To do that, click
"Search tools" beneath the search box (as indicated
by the arrow below).

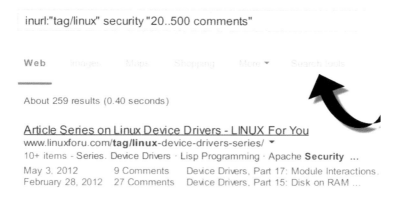

Additional options will appear. Mouse over the "Any
time" link and pick the time option you want.

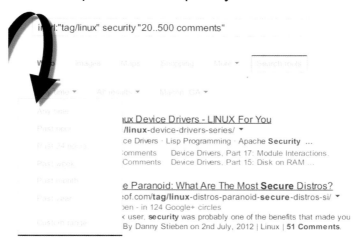

HOW TO FIND INDUSTRY RELATED CONTENT

Here are some Google searches [13] you can do to find industry related content that you may want to share. Namely, top resources curated by bloggers and passive candidates affiliated with the industry. For the sake of demonstration, let's put the focus on "cloud computing."

"cloud computing" intitle:top (resources OR articles OR websites)

...

"cloud computing" intitle:best intitle:tools

...

"cloud computing" (intitle:recommended OR intitle:favorite OR intitle:useful)

...

inanchor:"cloud computing" "interesting links"

...

intitle:"round up" "cloud computing"

...

(intitle:list OR intitle:promising) "cloud computing"

...

"cloud computing" intitle:"guide to"

...

---

[13] I am using advanced search operators in these examples. The "intitle" command searches for keywords in the title of a webpage. The "inanchor" command looks for a keyword in any type of link, title or url of a website. Notice that the word "OR" is capitalized. When searching Google or Bing or Yahoo in this way, "or" should be capitalized. "Inurl" finds keywords in the URL of a site.

inanchor:"cloud computing" intitle:"best of"

…

inurl:"cloud computing" intitle:"of 2013"

…

intitle:"cloud computing" intitle:most.popular

…

Okay, so I forgot something. A couple of pages ago I showed how to find blog posts with lots of comments. You can do a similar search to find forum discussions with lots of comments. Simply run a search along these lines:

"cloud computing" "10..25 comments"

When the results are returned, click the "More" link then, choose "Discussions" and Google will look only in online forums. How cool is that? I think its cool. ;-)

"cloud computing" "10..25 comments"

Web   Images   Maps   Shopping   More ▾   Search tools

About 6,380,000 results (0.50 seconds)

Ad related to **"cloud computing" "10..25 com**

Cloud Computing Services - Servers   her Cores
www.softlayer.com/Cloud ▾
Build Your Own & It's Up in Minutes
SoftLayer has 1,879 followers on Google+
Cloud Storage - Cloud Servers - Private Clouds   Discussions

Recipes

Alliance Revs Up **Cloud Computing** F   es
www.eetimes.com/author.asp?section_id=3   ▾
Oct 25, 2013 - Alliance Revs Up **Cloud Comp**   Ballingall
Director, ... **10 comments** post a comment. N   R

Okay, so back to finding industry related content. Let me turn your gaze to Twitter. Check out the search below. (Please note it only works on Twitter.)

#sourcing filter:links

My twitter search is looking for the hashtag "#sourcing" with the search results filtered so that I see only those results with a link included. Furthermore, you may notice in the screenshot below that I

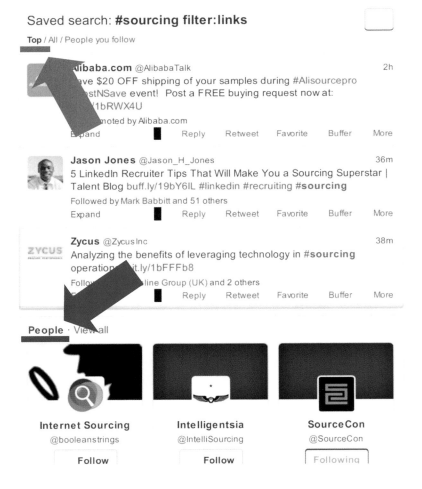

Saved search: **#sourcing filter:links**

Top / All / People you follow

Alibaba.com @AlibabaTalk   2h
Save $20 OFF shipping of your samples during #Alisourcepro
JustNSave event! Post a FREE buying request now at:
1bRWX4U
Promoted by Alibaba.com
Expand   Reply   Retweet   Favorite   Buffer   More

Jason Jones @Jason_H_Jones   36m
5 LinkedIn Recruiter Tips That Will Make You a Sourcing Superstar |
Talent Blog buff.ly/19bY6IL #linkedin #recruiting **#sourcing**
Followed by Mark Babbitt and 51 others
Expand   Reply   Retweet   Favorite   Buffer   More

Zycus @ZycusInc   38m
Analyzing the benefits of leveraging technology in **#sourcing**
operations it.ly/1bFFFb8
Followed by ...line Group (UK) and 2 others
                 Reply   Retweet   Favorite   Buffer   More

People · View all

Internet Sourcing   Intelligentsia   SourceCon
@booleanstrings   @IntelliSourcing   @SourceCon

    Follow   Follow   Following

underlined the word "top" in red (See the red arrow on the previous page?) When you do a search of any kind, by default, Twitter sorts the results and shares the most popular ones. Now I know what are the most popular links related to #sourcing on Twitter. Furthermore, if I scroll down the results page (where I underlined the "People" section in blue (See the blue arrow?), I see three Twitter accounts being featured. This tells me that @booleanstrings, @intellisourcing and @sourcecon are the most popular Tweeps (people on twitter) who discuss that hashtag. As such, I might want to follow them and see what they tweet about as I might want to share it. Make sense?

Now to make this search even more interesting, I add the term "RT" which stands for retweet. (A retweet is when you re-post something someone else has tweeted.) By doing the below search, Twitter will reveal the most popular tweets, with links that have been retweeted. This is how I would find links that are resonating with the audience following a hashtag. (wink)

#sourcing RT filter:links

Some websites are great for finding shareable content, but not so good at helping you figure out how that content is appealing to its audience. Fortunately, one can use Google to help discern that. Let me share a couple of examples of what I mean.

Slideshare.net is the world's largest community for sharing presentations. With 60 million monthly visitors and 130 million pageviews, it is amongst the most visited 200 websites in the world. Besides presentations, SlideShare also supports documents, PDFs, videos and webinars. (As per the Slideshare website.)

Slideshare has a search function that lets you track down content based on file type, when uploaded and a few other variables. However, one cannot search for content based on the popularity of the content producer which would suggest qualitative information. Fortunately, I can hack a search on Google to find this data.   Check out my search below.

site:slideshare.net "cloud computing"   "3000..5000 followers"

Some of the search results are below.

Jonathan Boutelle presentations channel - SlideShare
www.slideshare.net/jboutelle ▾
Jonathan Boutelle. Pro Account · Following Follow Processing... 56 SlideShares · **3832 Followers**. ×. Modal header. One fine body... Yes No. 480 2nd St Suite ...

Information Security in Retail & Consumer Goods - SlideShare
www.slideshare.net/.../information-security-in-retail-cg-ie-foundation-an... ▾
Oct 4, 2013 - An Essential Guide to Possibilities and Risks of **Cloud Computing**: A ...... Dunn was a particularly avid user of Twitter, with over **5,000 followers**.

Internet of Things - SlideShare
www.slideshare.net/CiscoIBSG/internet-of-things-8470978 ▾
Jun 30, 2011 - This tree has **3,000 followers** —do you? To view additional IBSG ... The Business Value of **Cloud Computing** 4323 views Like. Enterprise Video: ...

Amazon Web Services presentations channel - SlideShare
www.slideshare.net/AmazonWebServices/tagged/partner-presentation ▾
1174 SlideShares · **3736 Followers**. × ... 1 year ago, 1737 views; DLT - A Brave New World: Public Sector Strategies for Leveraging **Cloud Computing** DLT - A ...

And just for the sake of clarity, I am doing a search on the Slideshare website for pages that have the term "cloud computing" where the content producer has a following ranging from 3,000 to 5,000. Get me?

I can also modify the results to base my searches on comments generated and the number of likes that has been received. Here are a few search strings to spark your imagination.

site:slideshare.net "social media" twitter "500..5000 followers" "15..200 comments"

site:slideshare.net "chemical engineering" science "5..200 likes"

site:slideshare.net microsoft google facebook apple trends "mobile browser" "5..200 likes"

site:slideshare.net "mobile recruiting trends"

POP GOES THE CONTENT

Okay, one more tip before I switch topics. Another way to find content worth sharing is to check the most popular items featured on certain content aggregators. Here are a few that I frequent when seeking great information to share.

Alltop.com collects all the top headlines from popular subjects around the web. They cover topics of all sorts and (hopefully) what you recruit is included. As an example, I share a screenshot (next page) of how Alltop shares headlines from the world of Human Resources.

On the page is a list of headlines from popular blogs

focused on the HR industry. In the upper left hand of the section is a "Most Topular Stories" area (see arrow?) featuring the most popular of the popular headlines featured on this page.

Alltop seemed to be modeled after a website called Popurls.com which also aggregates headlines from leading blogs and divides them into topics. There are not as many subjects covered on Popurls as there are on Alltop. Just FYI…

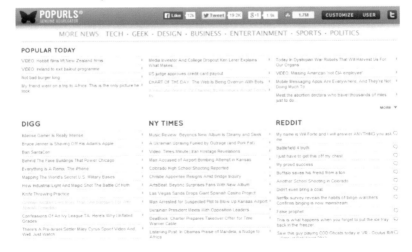

Techmeme.com tracks what tech news is trending across the web. What I like about it is how it will share a headline and then link to all the news sources that also carry the story as well. It really gives you insight into how far a story has traveled across the web.

The makers of Techmeme also produce similar sites like Mediagazer.com which focuses on the news media, Memeorandom.com (politics) and Wesmirch.com (celebrity gossip).

Another site I like for tech news is Newswhip.com.

Newswhip focuses on the world's emerging stories, so chances are you can find out the next big thing just as it starts to become the next big thing.

And last, but certainly not least, is LinkedIn's Pulse (www.linkedin.com/today). Pulse has more channels (I think) than Alltop or at least, is comparable to it. What is also compelling about Pulse is that you not only see what is trending in general across various topics but, from your LinkedIn homepage, you see what is trending among the people you are connected with as well. (Very cool.)

Below is Pulse as seen on the LinkedIn website. (There is a mobile app version as well.)

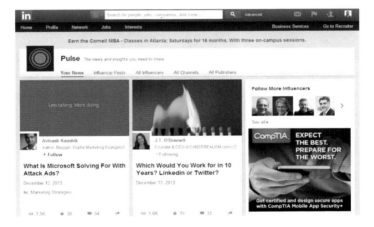

QUICK RECAP

To find quality content that you can share with your audience, you will have to do some research.

- Search blogs for popular posts
- Search Twitter for popular links and retweets

- Take a gander at Slideshare for content from its most popular producers.
- Review sites that curate content from leading blogs like Alltop and Popurls.

Finding quality content to share with your audience is great! However, nothing beats creating your own stuff. If its good, and all your content should be very, very good, then it will get shared and help to increase your audience which will (of course) send more passive candidates your way.

What I want to do now is suggest a few strategies that can inspire **content development**.

QUESTIONS AND ANSWER SITES

Are you familiar with "Question and Answer" sites? They are online forums where people ask questions and other people answer them. Go figure. One of the more popular of these types of websites is "Quora."

I highly recommend checking out Quora and search-ing for keywords related to your recruiting interests. In the results you will find the most popular questions on the Quora website related to those keywords and that should give you some idea on what the people you want to attract might want to know more about.

For demo purposes I searched Quora for questions related to Natural Language Processing (as shown on the next page). The most popular question is "What are the most important research papers which all NLP students should definitely read?" Among the answers are at lest ten suggestions. If you were recruiting people in the NLP field, based on this, a blog post might be, "10 Research Papers NLP Students Must Read Today."

Once you posted your content, there will be some who agree and disagree with your list. Take note of all of them as they all are potential hires. Make sense?

Results for "natural language processing"

Natural
Language
Processing

Natural Language Processing   [Follow]

Natural Language Processing refers to the use of computers to analyze
natural language for any number of purposes. It's almost the same as
Computational Linguistics - see W... (more)
Topic: Top Stories · Questions

★ **What are the most important research papers which all NLP students should definitely read?**

Graham Neubig, Grad Student studying NLP, particularly Unsupervised Learning for Machine Translation and other A... (more)   102

Votes by Zoltan Varju, Christopher Lin, Yusuke Matsubara, Masato Hagiwara, and 97 more.

I honestly think that there is no single *research paper* that every NLPer should read. NLP is such a broad field that no person can specialize in everything, and research papers are, by nature, rather narrowly focused.

Here are a few more question and answer sites you might want to consider adding to your bag of tricks. I like these sites especially because their members have profile pages and/or a means to contact them personally and that makes it easier to connect to them privately.

- Yahoo Answers (answers.yahoo.com)
- Answers (www.answers.com)
- AolAnswers (www.aolanswers.com)
- Answerbag (www.answerbag.com)
- AllExperts (www.allexperts.com)

ANOTHER "SUGGESTION"

Do you know what Google Suggest is? Chances are that you use it quite often; you just did not know you were! Google's Search Suggest automatically recommends popular searches as you type your query into the search field. [14]

Google | What is google sugg|est
what is google sugg**est** Remove
what is google sugg**est keyword tool**
what is google sugg**estions based on**
what is google sugg**ested sites**

Let's say you wanted to target software engineers with your content. One of the suggested searches that appears when looking for "software engineers" is "software engineering code of ethics." (as seen below) Such being the case, a blog post on that topic could attract a lot of readers who are searching for information on that topic.

Google | software eng
software eng**ineer**
software eng**ineer salary**
software eng**ineering code of ethics**
software eng**ineer job description**

Suggested searches to try:
- Keywords and phrases from the job description
- Search variations of job titles
- Add question phrases like "how to," "what is," and "where is" in front of keywords

[14] For extra credit, look up "keyword research tools."

Additional searches to try are below. Of course, change the job title "programmer" to whatever fits your needs.

- programmers love it
- programmers hate this
- Is popular with programmers
- drives programmers crazy
- best thing about being a programmer
- worst thing about being a programmer
- "as a programmer" (love OR hate)

TOO BUSY TO PRODUCE CONTENT?

Here are a few ways you can produce content when time is an issue.

QUOTES: Blog posts focused on quotes tend to do well in terms of garnering attention and are certainly easy to create. All you have to do is add a few introductory words to begin your post, add a list of quotes and then a few words concluding your post.

To find quotes to cite in your blog post, simply do a few Google searches as I have done. (Shared below) Simply change the bolded keywords I am using to something that fits your needs.

- Quotes on **accounting**
- famous words of wisdom about **dentistry**
- "**CEO** of" "quoted as saying"
- "at **microsoft** is quoted as saying"
- quotes about being an **administrative assistant**

INTERVIEWS: A post where you interview someone

is a win-win all around. You get content that you didn't have to write, the profile of the interviewee is raised and your readers get a fresh perspective. One method of interviewing is to simply send a list of questions that you want the interviewee to answer. Once you have their responses, write a short introductory text, add the interviewee's information and badda-boom-badda-bing, all done. And just as a FYI, this goes over well with the interviewee because they can take his or her time to give a "perfect" answer.

Another interview method that takes a bit more time and a little more work, is to record a conference call (or in-person conversation) and post it online. Here are a few tools you might want to use when considering this path.

- freeconferencecall.com
- audioboo.fm
- soundcloud.com

POLLS: Simply ask a question and let your readers respond. For this to work best, you want your question to be thought-provoking and controversial. Of course, you can also ask a question that would benefit people in their everyday work life. For example: http://buff.ly/IQ1SXP

Something else you can do along these lines is to research twitter on a topic, embed tweets you think are controversial and ask your readers to chime in on the comments.

RECAPS: Go through your archives and find an article that was once popular. Re-post it with updated information. Easy-peasy. You could also opt to review your archives and create a list of your most popular blog posts for the year and make that a blog post. Once again, easy-peasy.

A PICTURE IS WORTH A THOUSAND WORDS (...AND A FEW HIRES)

Do you have a smartphone? comScore says 62.5% of Americans have one (149.2 million users) and Business Insider recently cited a statistic from their research which says 1 in every 5 people in the world own a smartphone. And can you guess what is happening on all of these phones? Of course, people are making calls on them. You know what else? Pictures. Lots and lots of pictures.

The number one activity on Facebook is uploading and sharing photos. Next to tweeting a comment, up-loading and sharing photos is what people are doing on Twitter. And on Google Plus, uploading and sharing photos is... yeah, you guessed it, the number one activity. Are you sensing a pattern here? [15]

Pictures are hot on the internet and I believe they will remain so. Pictures speak to short attention spans and that is especially appreciated in this information overload society. Plus, they are known to increase audience engagement (photos that elicit an emotional response work best) and if you describe them well enough, you may get a boost of visibility in the search engine results.

[15] 12 Awesome Social Media Facts and Statistics for 2013
http://buff.ly/IR5kBz

All that being said, I want to share with you strategies for leveraging pictures as content.

COMICS

There are several products that you can leverage to make cartoons online. One of the more popular ones is called - Bitstrips. (www.bitstrips.com)

What are these comics and why are they taking over my feed!?

How cool would it be to create a comic strip series based on what its like to work for your company? I think it would be very cool and could potentially go viral. You could also try using comics to answer frequently asked questions, give interview tips or to share funny moments from the office that passive candidates might appreciate. Just a thought.

SHOUT OUT TO EMPLOYEES

Photos are a good way to showcase employees and prove to passive candidates how valued your workers are. Recently promoted employees, recipients of a company award, community outreach of some kind or, fun at a company event would all be great excuses to share photos across social media.

QUOTABLES

I mentioned earlier how you could create content by listing a series of quotes. (pg 40) You could easily turn quotes into photographic works of art by using a cool tool - Recite This. (www.recitethis.com)

Basically, how it works is that you type in a few words, choose your background and "Recite This" gives you links where you can download the picture you created or share it across various networks.

DESIGN FOR THE PLATFORM

Create profile pictures that Facebook users can adopt. No doubt, you have seen these on Facebook where there is an arrow pointing to a user's name or, perhaps a cover image pointing to a profile picture? In either case, these types of pictures tend to spread and that can be of great benefit to your company.

Should you go this route, I want to suggest that you add a URL on the image in some way. This will make it easy for others to find the website you are promoting.

Here are a couple of examples to accent my point. The first visual (shown below) [16] is a Facebook profile picture and the second is Facebook cover. [17] Hopefully, both will inspire creativity within you.

Because you matter! 6 of 6   Options   Share   Send   Like

[16] Picture profile source: "Because you matter!" http://buff.ly/1fkK3uL
[17] Pet Super Adoption Timeline Cover Photos http://buff.ly/1fkKxAS

POST PHOTOS AS LINKS

Photos have a huge Edgerank, so why not take advantage of this and use photos as links to other content you produce? But, before I get into that, allow me a moment for a quick tangent.

Edgerank is an algorithm developed by Facebook to govern what is displayed - and how high - on the News feed. [18] What has traditionally affected Edgerank has changed over the years and now there are more factors. Actually, the term Edgerank is no longer used internally at Facebook itself. [19] I use the term here, only because I am used to saying it. Okay, tangent over.

Now, where was I? (Let me scan up a few lines...) Ah! Okay. To post photos as links, follow these steps.

- Select a great photo that best represents a piece of content you have online. Ideally, it is a large photo with great resolution.

[18] What Is EdgeRank? http://buff.ly/1fkPrOw
[19] EdgeRank Is Dead: Facebook's News Feed Algorithm Now Has Close To 100K Weight Factors http://buff.ly/1fkPyJW

- Post the picture on Facebook.
- In the "Add a description" section, post a short description about the content you are citing along with a link to said content.

Chances are people will share, comment, like and generally engage with a post with a great visual and a link than a post with a link only. Below is an example of this strategy in action.

CROWDSOURCE PHOTO CAPTIONS

Photo caption posts inspire imagination and certainly encourage interaction from those following your brand. When producing a photo caption post, think about the emotion you want to trigger and the type of messages people might respond with. You want to use an image that is irresistible along with a good description that invites fans to engage.

As an extra bit of enticement, make it a contest. Here is an example of what I mean.

...

Help me caption this photo by walknboston [20]. Tweet your suggestions to me @jimstroud with the hashtag #ribbit. The best captions will be awarded one milllion dollars in imaginary money and (maybe) a retweet. How exciting is that?!

You can find and use photos from a variety sources

online and not have to worry about copyright issues. [21]

PHOTOS INTO VIDEO

Have you heard of Animoto? (www.animoto.com) They let you make videos by simply uploading pictures, choosing music and adding text. After you have identified your preferences of music and text, Animoto adds some Hollywood special effects and in moments, a video is ready to be shared.

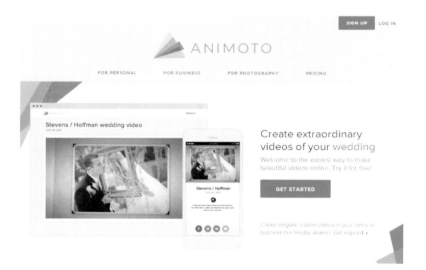

They offer free and premium services. I have used both and give them the thumbs up. Just sayin'...

You know, while I am on the topic of videos, let me

[21] **Flickr Creative Commons** - www.flickr.com/creativecommons/ **Shutterstock** - www.shutterstock.com/   **iStock** - www.istockphoto.com **Photo Pin** - www.photopin.com

share a few words about Vine.

VIDEO MADE EASY

Are you hip to Vine? For those who don't know, Vine is a free mobile application that enables users to record and share an unlimited number of short, looping video clips with a maximum length of six seconds. Vine is owned by Twitter.

You might think that six seconds is not long enough to make a video of any worth. If that is your thinking, I suggest you do a bit of research to see how brands are using Vine videos to promote their brand. [22]

I think Vine opens up a lot of possibilities. For one, there is the SEO advantage and that alone is pretty major. SEO stands for "search engine optimiza-tion" (Did I say that already?) which is the process of affecting the visibility of a web page in search results. Google loves video when it comes to search engine ranking and I saw this first hand. Mind if I go off on another tangent?

TRIP DOWN MEMORY LANE

Back in the day, I was on Microsoft's International Recruiting Team. In that role, I sourced software engineers for various positions all over the world. To attract passive candidates, I used a Flip camera (Less than $100 expense at the time) to record a recruiting video and Windows Movie Maker (free software that comes with a PC) to edit said video.

[22] How To Use Twitter's Vine for Recruiting - YouTube http://buff.ly/1hXlZi0
Why my recruiting video ranks higher than Twitter's recruiting video | The Recruiters Lounge http://buff.ly/1hXJ2KJ

From start to finish, it took me about 4 hours (give or take) to get it all done. I produced the video in 2007 but, it is still paying off big dividends for Microsoft. Check out what happens when you do a search for "Microsoft Canada Development Center." Page one search results! [23]

---

microsoft canada development center

Web   Images   Maps   Shopping   Videos   More ▼   Search tools

---

About 33,000,000 results (0.21 seconds)

Vancouver **Development Center - Microsoft**
www.**microsoft**.com/en-ca/corp/vdc/ ▼
The Vancouver **Development Center** (VDC) is located in Vancouver, British Columbia,
Canada. The centre is home to some of the best and brightest software ...
Work @ VDC · Life @ VDC · Careers @ VDC · Contact Us

Canada Development Centre - Microsoft.com
careers.**microsoft**.com/careers/en/ca/**developmentcentre**.aspx ▼
Since opening its doors in September 2007, the MCDC has quickly become an intricate
part of **Microsoft's** global strategy for distributed software **development**.

Microsoft Careers: Our Office Locations
careers.**microsoft**.com/careers/en/ca/offices.aspx ▼
In addition, the **Microsoft Canada Development Centre** (MCDC) in Richmond, British
Columbia plays a key role in architecting systems, developing code, and ...

Microsoft Canadian Development Centre - Jobs at Microsoft
www.**microsoft**-careers.com/.../**Microsoft-Canadian-Development-Centre**... ▼
Microsoft Canadian Development Centre. Since opening its doors in September
2007, the MCDC has quickly become an intricate part of Microsoft's global ...

Life at **Microsoft's Canada Development Center** - YouTube

www.youtube.com/watch?v=zF92y_wiN_U ▼
Jan 9, 2008 - Uploaded by MicrosoftRecruiter
Hi, my name is Jim Stroud (jstroud@**microsoft**.com) and I am a
member of **Microsoft's** International ...

---

[23] My search was done in "Incognito" mode which means that they were not personalized to me. (For the sake of those who were wondering.) Also, I uploaded my video first on Vimeo in November 2007. That video is on page 2. I uploaded it later to YouTube in January 2008. Hmm... Is Google giving preference to YouTube over Vimeo? What are the odds of that?

I also get page one ranking on Yahoo, Bing, Ask and AOL Search for the same term. What this means is when someone is researching the Microsoft Canada Development Center, my video will be on page one of the search results. And such has been the case since 2007! How much did I pay for that? (Or rather, Microsoft?) Nothing! Unless you count the four hours it took me to put it all together and upload it.

Now, consider the four hours (give or take) to make a ten minute video verses the effort it takes to produce a six second Vine video. When it comes to SEO, the result could be the same because despite the length, its still a video. Is the lightbulb blinking over your head now?

A FEW VINE IDEAS FOR YOU

- On the Vine app is a section called "On the Rise" which showcases Vines that are trending up- wards in popularity. See if there are any videos there that you can add to a blog post to attract more attention to your content.
- Use Vine to post very short announcements on Twitter and ask your followers to retweet it. For example, a recruiter could say, "We're having a career fair. Details in the comments." Of course, add a URL in the description pointing to more information as well as more data in the comments.
- Vine videos are being indexed by Google. [24] Use relevant hashtags to increase the chances of your Vines being seen outside of the network of those following you.

[24] Google Search http://buff.ly/1cpx6f6

- Showcase the culture of your company by posting Vines of everyday activities there. For example, highlights from a charitable initiative, office party or workplace hijinks.
- Is your company presenting at a conference? Why not post Vines showcasing your presenter in action?
- You can sign up for a Vine vanity url like mine: www.vine.co/JimStroud Once you have one, add it to your email signature and spread the word about your Vine content. No worries on costs. It's a freebie. Simply sign into your Vine account online (www.vine.co) and follow the instructions there. By the way, feel free to follow me on Vine as well. It will incentivize me to produce more content there. (smile)

I've shared a few ways to produce content quickly and easily. However, what's the use of making

[25] Shown above is my profile on Vine.

content if no one consumes it? Such being the case, I want to switch gears a bit and direct you to ways that will increase the chances of your content being seen. Okeedokee? Here we go.

CURRENT EVENTS

One sure fire way to get your content viewed is to tie it to a current event or upward trend. Here are some resources to assist you in finding such.

- **Google News** [news.google.com] is a source of news that you can personalize to your tastes. For example, imagine that you have an interest in software engineering. You can either add the search to your Google News homepage (as shown below) or have an email alert sent to you. (As demonstrated on the following page.)

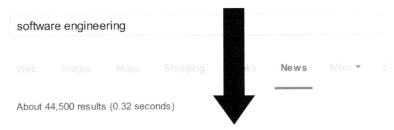

software engineering

Web   Images   Maps   Shopping   ks   **News**   More ▾

About 44,500 results (0.32 seconds)

Add "**software engineering**" section to my Google News homepage

What Was It Like To Be A **Software Engineer** At NeXT?
Forbes · Dec 17, 2013
NeXT was like graduate school, bringing together a high concentration of some of the brightest and most innovative technical minds.

Senior **Software Engineer** - Embedded/Driver Development
ElectronicsWeekly.com · 16 hours ago
An exciting opportunity has arisen for a Senior **Software Engineer** to join a leading consumer electronics developer based near Watford. This is ...

Bachelor & Assoc Degree Programs in **Engineering** Tech. Get More Info!

Internationally known company in Essex with expanding product range now seeks a skilled Senior Embedded **Software Engineer**. Applicants ...

Stay up to date on these results:

- Create an email alert for **software engineering**

1 2 3 4 5 6 7 8 9 10   Next

The se ... and placement of stories on this page were determined automatically by a computer program ... he or date displayed reflects when an article was added to or updated in Google News.

- You can monitor trends on **Twitter** in at least two ways that I am aware. One way is to view the trends displayed on Twitter itself. (See below.) They are shown on the left hand side of a Twitter profile.

- Another way is via a cool tool called - **Trendsmap**. [www.trendsmap.com] Trendsmap shows the most popular hashtags on a map. As such, you can see what is trending at certain locations at a glance. There are free and premium versions of this service.
- **Yahoo! News Trending Now** is another resource [news.yahoo.com/blogs/trending-now/] for finding increasingly popular news and content.

- **Google Trends** [www.google.com/trends/] shows you what searches are being conducted en masse.
- **Trending Topics** [http://www.trendingtopics.org/] shows what Wikipedia topics are growing in popularity.
- **Rebloggy** [www.rebloggy.com] shows you the top posts on Tumblr.com.
- **YouTube Trends Dashboard** [youtube.com/trendsdashboard] and **YouTube Trendsmap** [youtube.com/trendsmap] both show you what is popular on YouTube at the moment with target demographics.

EMBEDDABLE CONTENT

Another way to boost readership of the content you have posted on social networks is to repost it on a blog or website. Many of the social networks allow you to embed content from their site. Here is a list of the ones that immediately come to mind.

- Google Plus
- Facebook
- Twitter
- Instagram
- Flickr
- Vine
- Storify
- Soundcloud
- Google Docs
- Scribd
- Slideshare
- YouTube

Each network has its own way of doing things, but essentially they operate the same way. You pick out content, get the web code needed to post the content and then add it to your blog or website. For demo purposes, I will show you how to embed content from Facebook.

With Facebook, you can embed public posts from personal profiles or pages. To do so, go to your news feed, profile or page and click on the drop-down arrow at the top right of the post. You'll see the option to embed the post. (See below.)

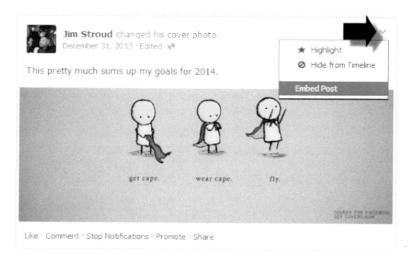

When you click on the "Embed Post" link, a pop-up window will appear with embed code. Copy that code and place it on your website or blog, where you want the content to appear. (Shown on next page.)

...

Now I want to share two ideas on using embeddable content on your blog or website to promote your employment brand and attract passive candidates.

Embed this Post   ×

`<div id="fb-root"></div> <script>(function(d, s, id) { var js, fjs = d.ge`

Copy and paste this code into your website. Learn More

Preview: Width (px): 466

Jim Stroud
Entrepreneur at Jim Stroud, Inc.   330 followers

Timeline ▼

This pretty much sums up my goals for 2014

get cape.   wear cape.   fly.

Below is an example of a worker tweeting a positive message about their employer. If the tweet below was about your company, I would suggest that you retweet it, then embed it into a blog post and discuss it further. Make sense? Maybe even search for multiple comments like this and entitle your post, "What people are saying about us on Twitter."

Scott Ellis
@blahblahellis

I love working at Fairfax! What other company would allow its own employees a forum to attack their policies?
theage.com.au/business/how-h...

If your company has a page on Google Plus, you could post tips on how to interview at your company (as Google has done) then, embed that post on a company blog. This gives your blog content and lets your blog audience know that you also have a Google Plus page that they could be following.

Have a Pinterest board? A Twitter account? The same strategy applies with them as well.

Life at Google
Shared publicly · Oct 11, 2012

If you missed Tuesday's candidate coaching session on Tech interviewing at Google, the recording is now up on our YouTube channel. Here's the rundown:

0:00 - Introductions
0:59 - How we hire Software Engineers
2:49 - Interview preparation
11:38 - Working through sample interview question
26:10 - Example solution
32:59 - Answering user questions

If you're interested in applying for one of our engineering roles, please visit our job site: http://goo.gl/2FbS7

+190   ⤴93

AND NOW, A FEW WORDS ON INSTAGRAM

Do you know about Instagram? Chances are that you are well aware of it, but for the sake of those who do not know anything about it, here is what you need to know.

Instagram is an online photo-sharing, video-sharing and social networking service that enables its users to take pictures and videos, apply digital filters to them, and share them on a variety of social networking services, such as Facebook, Twitter, Tumblr and Flickr. It has 150+ million users, 1 billion photos are shared on it daily and Facebook acquired it for a billion dollars in 2012. (Thus concludes your crash course on Instagram.)

At this writing, it does not look like too many companies are using Instagram to promote their employment brand. This gives you a strategic advantage. [26]

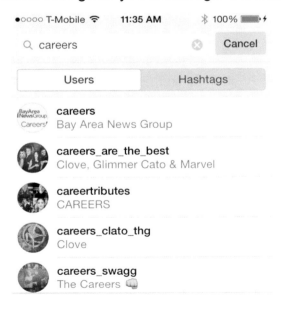

While I applaud the efforts, there are engagement practices by some Instagram accounts that I am not a fan of. Let me share a few with you.

- 15 Seconds of someone reading a job description (@jobs_hiring_in_philly)
- Images of job titles above a recruiter's email address. (@jobs_in_kuwait)
- An account made exclusively of clip art. (@jobscouting)
- Spam in the comments of photos pointing to a website. Why not delete the spam? Are they not monitoring their own account? (@jobscouting)
- Images of partial job descriptions with links to the full job description n the comments section of the photo. (@jobsinjordan)
- Accounts without websites associated with them or a clear mission statement. (@jobsinthed)
- Accounts with several pictures that looked the same. (@jobs4bahrainis)

Again, let me say how much I appreciate their forward thinking because even if I disagree with their approach, I salute them because they are FAR ahead of so many others who are not even trying. Just to put it out there. So, please don't hate me. :-)

A FEW INSTAGRAM STRATEGIES I LIKE

- Have a distinctive user logo to differentiate between consumer brand and employment brand. Be sure to have a clear statement of who you are and a link to a career site. [27]

[26] On the previous page is an image of an Instagram search of users.
[27] Check out the differences between the images shared on the next page.

marrrottcareers ·

Marriott Jobs and Careers 1100 managed locations, 75 countries and 18 brands means the career opportunities with Marriott are endless. Find your world. http://jobs.marriott.com

Follow

182	492	304
posts	followers	following

Adding a hashtag to the bio provides an additional advantage as it allows you to share your most recent marketing campaigns. At least, those campaigns with an associated hashtag.

marriotthotels ·

Marriott Hotels & Resorts Marriott is on a journey to make travel uncomplicated. Unforgettable. Brilliant. Create the future of travel with us. #TravelBrilliantly http://www.travelbrilliantly.com

Follow

472	5,719	53
posts	followers	following

- Create a content strategy around what you plan to share on Instagram. Consider questions like: a) Who are you trying to attract? b) What would best express your company culture? c) What hashtags could you create or dominate? d) What events or promotions do you want to share? e) How can you showcase your employees?

- Make branded photos on the cheap and share them on Instagram. There is an iphone app called "**Instajob**" ($0.99) that lets you quickly add text over an image. What one could do is take a picture of an empty cubicle, add text like "Now Hiring Engineers" and a link to your careers website. [www.careercloud.com/instajob/]

AN INSTAGRAM EXPERIMENT

I confess that at this writing, I have not had a reason to fully implement this strategy. Should you do so, please let me know how it has worked for you. I believe it will work. Okay, here it goes. What you may have noticed on Instagram accounts is that people often add their job titles to their bios on Instagram.

Now imagine that you wanted to target an audience of software engineers on Instagram. You would start by doing a Google search along these lines.

site:instagram.com "software developer"

Among the search results is "Eric Silva who has identified himself as a Software Developer. (Search result shown below.)

ericjsilva's Profile • Instagram
instagram.com/ericjsilva ▾
Eric Silva **Software developer**. Dad. Photographer. Scoutmaster. Geek. Nerd. I like math, donuts, coffee, Mt. Dew, owls, and 80s music. http://ericsilva.org · Log in.

When I click the link to his Instagram profile, I see that there is a link to a blog he produces. Good to know but, that's not my focus. (Image on next page.)

ericjsilva ·

Eric Silva Software developer. Dad. Photographer. Scout master. Geek. Nerd. I like math, donuts, coffee, Mt. Dew, owls, and 80s music. http://ericsilva.org

Follow

161 posts   38 followers   49 following

Using the Instagram mobile app,   I send Eric a picture via **Instagram Direct** with the hope that it gets his attention and sparks a conversation that results in my recruiting him into my company.

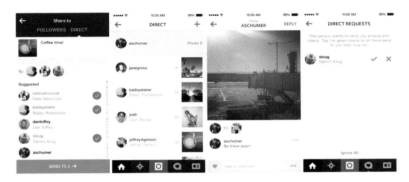

Here are instructions from the Instagram blog. [28] *"When you open Instagram, you'll now see a new icon in the top right corner of your home feed. Tap it to open your inbox where you'll see photos and videos that people have sent to you. To send a photo or video to specific people, tap the camera button to enter the same simple photo or video capture and editing screens. At the top of the share screen, you'll*

see the option to share with your followers ("Followers") or to send to specific people ("Direct"). To send using Direct, tap the names of the people you want to send your photo or video to, write your caption, tap "send" and you're done. After sending, you'll be able to find out who's seen your photo or video, see who's liked it and watch your recipients commenting in real time as the conversation unfolds."

In this case, I have chosen to send one message to one person (Eric J. Silva). I could however, elect to send one message to as many as fifteen users at a time. An alternative strategy is to tag photos that you want brought to the attention of certain users. The advantage of this tactic is that the followers of the user you are targeting might see your photo as well. Check out the step by step instructions below.)

| Take a photo and tag someone you want to recruit. | Maybe the photo promotes the company culture in some way? | Once photo is tagged, the person is notified. | Tagged photos are added to a "Photos of (Username)" section. Unless user turns it off, your photo could be seen by that user's network. |

[28] Introducing Instagram Direct - http://buff.ly/1khvT3R

KNOW YOUR ENEMY, KNOW YOURSELF

On to another topic now, just to keep you on your toes. (smile)

Employment branding is the practice of managing your firm's image or reputation as an excellent place to work. Before you develop your content and certainly prior to it getting seen, I suggest that you perform an employer brand audit. In other words, get to know how your employer brand is perceived by the public. Once that is done, it is also to your benefit to gauge how your competitors are seen in the eyes of passive candidates as well. When you are trying to close candidates, such knowledge can be crucial.

All that being said, what is your company culture? How is it regarded internally? Does it really match up to the verbiage on your company website? Use a tool like Surveymonkey [www.surveymonkey.com] to poll those in your company. Below are some questions you might want to consider posing.

How many years have you worked at (company)?
- <1
- 1-3
- 3-5
- 5+

Has (company) developed a clear Employer Branding Strategy?
- Yes, we have a clear strategy
- Yes, but it can be further developed
- No, we do not have a strategy
- I don't know

Which activities is (company) currently undertaking to enhance your employer brand? (please choose one or more responses)
- Alumni Program
- Career Website Development
- Coaching / Mentoring
- Defining Employer Value Proposition
- Employee Referral Program
- Focus group of current employees to define employer brand
- Leadership Development Program
- Mobile Careers Site
- Retention Initiatives
- Social Media Outreach
- I don't know

How important do you believe the following employer brand attributes are in attracting new talent to your company? Please rank from "least important" to "most important."
- Career development
- Compensation and benefits
- Corporate reputation and culture
- Corporate Social Responsibility
- Innovation
- Leadership
- Mission, vision, values
- People management practices and policies
- Performance management
- Recruitment and induction processes
- Reward and recognition
- Work environment

[continued on next page]

Which of the following is most important to you?
(Please choose one or more responses.)
- It is important to me that my friends know the company I work for
- My friends' perception of the company I work for is important
- It is important to me that my family knows the company I work for
- My family's perception of the company I work for is important
- It is important that other people want to work for my employer
- Other people's perception of the company that I work for is important to me.
- None of the above

Which activity has been most effective in enhancing your company's employer brand? (Choose one)
- Building an effective leadership development program
- Employee referral program
- Career website development
- Company videos
- Green efforts that reduce our carbon footprint
- Defining our employer value propositions (EVP's)
- Increased communications between our internal departments
- Introducing policies which encourage improved work flexibility
- Our ranking in Best Places to Work
- Salary increases
- Social media participation
- Talent pool development
- I don't know
- Other (please specify)

My hope is that in surveying your company internally, you will spark enough of a conversation that a clear vision of your company brand is articulated. Umm... In case you did not have one before. Of course, no matter your best intentions, its all for nothing if your communications are not being received as you planned them to be. Here are some ways you can check how people are discussing your employer brand online.

For the sake of demoing (and since I am a huge fan of their product), I will use Netflix as an example. A Google search on "What is it like to work at Netflix?" will reveal links to online forums where people are discussing that topic. (See below.)

what is it like to work at netflix

Web   Images   Maps   Shopping   More ▾   Search tools

About 176,000,000 results (0.72 seconds)

Working at **Netflix** | Glassdoor
www.glassdoor.com/.../**Work**ing-at-**Netflix**-EI_IE11891.11,18.htm ▾
Dec 26, 2013 - See what employees say it's **like to work at Netflix**. Salaries, reviews, and more - all posted by employees working at Netflix.

Working at **Netflix** | Indeed.com
www.indeed.com/cmp/**Netflix**/forums ▾
Rating: 3.3 - 69 reviews
What it's **like to work at Netflix**, and how to get hired - from Netflix Employees. Ask questions, get answers. Indeed.com.

Netflix Employee Reviews | Indeed.com
www.indeed.com/cmp/**Netflix**/reviews ▾
Rating: 3.3 - 69 reviews
Netflix Employer Reviews ... A typical IT job: Our goal is A, so we **want** you to do B.. ... The **work** I did for **Netflix** was very fast paced and sometimes we had very ...

Is this the only search you should do? Certainly not!

GOOGLE SEARCHES FOR MONITORING YOUR EMPLOYER BRAND

What are passive candidates and current employees saying about Netflix?
- I love working at Netflix
- I hate working at Netflix
- Working for Netflix
- Netflix interview questions
- How to get a job at Netflix
- Is Netflix a good place to work?

What does Netflix (really) care about?
- " Netflix is sponsoring * "
- " Netflix has invested in * "
- " Netflix supports * "
- " Netflix stands with * "

In addition to the searches above, take advantage of Google suggest to see how the crowd is researching topics related to your interest. By typing "Netflix supports" in the Google search bar, Google suggests additional keywords based on the searches of others.

netflix supports
netflix supports
netflix supports **sopa**
netflix supports **rush limbaugh**
netflix supports **limbaugh**

netflix charity
netflix charity
netflix charity **work**
netflix charity **donations**
netflix charity **love links**

You should also check Twitter to see who is happily (or angrily) discussing your company, depending on the smilee face you use.

Results for **"working at netflix"** :-)

Top / All / People you follow

Ismael Burciaga @burciaga   13 Apr
If it weren't for God's awesome plan, I would've been living in Los Gatos, California right now **working at Netflix** :-)
#onlyHeknowswhatsbest
⦿ from Grapevine, T   ← Reply ⇄ Retweet ★ Favorite ≋ Buffer ••• More

Captain Tech Support @MightyGeek   6 Jun 11
1st day **working at Netflix** today. It was pretty awesome. My employee account gets 8 discs at a time for free :) I can deal with that
Expand   ← Reply ⇄ Retweet ★ Favorite ≋ Buffer ••• More

jodi henderson @julesandjemma   3 Sep 10
RT @TelegraphNews http://bit.ly/blMsAN < fantastic! I should look into **working at Netflix**.... :-)
Followed by Will Staney and 1 other
Expand   ← Reply ⇄ Retweet ★ Favorite ≋ Buffer ••• More

Results for **"working at"** nursing :(

Top / All / People you follow

kattteeelllyynnn @katederpp   8h
The worst thing about **working at** a **nursing** home is when your favorite residents pass away :(
Expand   ▮   Reply   Retweet   Favorite   Buffer   More

Sample searches you can try on Twitter:
- (love OR hate) "working at" microsoft
- #work "at microsoft"
- Cisco "working on"
- "love my job" "your company name"
- "hate my job" "your company name"
- "hate working at" "your company name"

I want to share a couple of more tactics for research-ing your employment brand. First, search for popular blog posts that discuss your company. Here are a couple of search examples for your review.

inurl:tag/northrop.grumman "20..500 comments"

Web   Images   Maps   Shopping   More ▾   Search tools

About 12 results (0.31 seconds)

USNI Blog » northrop grumman
blog.usni.org/**tag/northrop-grumman** ▾
... in Navy | 5 Comments. Posted by Defense Springboard in Navy | 3 Comments. Posted by Defense Springboard in Coast Guard, Navy | **33 Comments**.

Northrop Grumman « Breaking Defense - Defense industry news ...
breakingdefense.com/**tag/northrop-grumman**/ ▾
Oct 8, 2013 - inShare. 5 Comments. 2 Comments. 6 Comments. 10 Comments. 1 Comment. **188 Comments**. 1 Comment. 5 Comments. **338 Comments**.

Northrop Grumman « Above the Law: A Legal Web Site – News ...

abovethelaw.com/**tag/northrop-grumman**/ ▾
by David Lat - in 180 Google+ circles
28 Comments · Share · Print. Tags: 7th Circuit, Appeals, Appellate Advocacy, Appellate Law, Benchslap, Benchslaps, Boyle Law Group, Bridget Boyle-Saxton, ...

In the search above, I am asking Google to look for blog posts that have been tagged with the phrase "Northrop Grumman" and have anywhere from 20 comments to 500 comments.

inurl:tag/salesforce "10..1000 comments"

The above search is doing a similar search, but focused on the company "salesforce" and blog posts with 10 to 1000 comments.

Web   Images   Maps   Shopping   More ▾   Search tools

10 results (0.30 seconds)

Housing & Transit | IBM Future Blue Canada
futureblue.wordpress.com/housing-and-student-accommodation/ ▾
10 Comments on "Housing & Transit" ... I'm Daniel Hu from the University of Waterloo
and I will be **working at IBM**/Cognos with a 90% chance at Ottawa and 10% ...

Release Of 9/11 Report Redacts Everything Israel Special Forces ...
emsnews.wordpress.com/.../release-of-911-report-redacts-everything-isra... ▾
Dec 27, 2013 - He attended the Technion – Israel Institute of Technology in Haifa while
simultaneously **working at IBM's** research laboratory .... **22 Comments**.

Industry vs. academia | Random bits
jonkatz.wordpress.com/2009/09/10/industry-vs-academia/ ▾
Sep 10, 2009 - I was on sabbatical last year, **working at IBM** Watson, and also had the
chance to make short visits to MSR New England, Google NY, and...

This search finds Wordpress blogs with 10 - 200 comments where the phrase "working at IBM" is mentioned. You can try this same search on other blog platforms besides Wordpress. Simply change the search parameter from site:wordpress.com to another domain like site:blogger.com. Everything else in the search string remains the same. Here is a list of other blog platforms you can experiment with on your searches.

- Blogger.com
- LiveJournal.com
- Squarespace.com
- Typepad.com
- Tumblr.com
- Blog.com
- Weebly.com

The bigger your company, the more likely you are to

find data on a blog search. Just FYI.

A great resource for employment brand research is Glassdoor. [www.glassdoor.com] Among other things, Glassdoor has a forum where workers rant and rave about their employers.

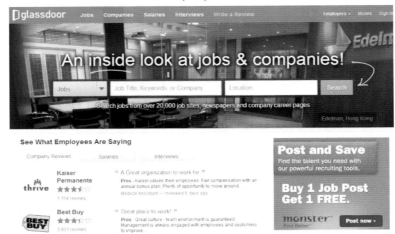

The job board Indeed has a forum where workers discuss their employers as well. Its not as robust as Glassdoor, but certainly worth a look. [www.indeed.com/forum/cmp]

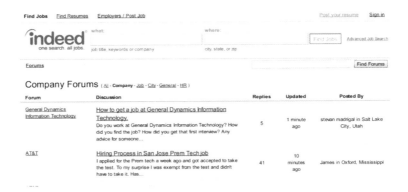

After doing so much research on yourself, use the same techniques on your closest competitors; everything but the survey of course. Use the information to create a SWOT analysis. (SWOT stands for strengths, weaknesses, opportunities and threats). Oh, waitasec, we did that back on page 21. My bad.

I've said a lot and I might be losing track myself, so let me do a quick recap since the last quick recap.

QUICK RECAP

- Use Q & A sites, Google Suggest, quotes, interviews and polls to generate content ideas.
- Sharing pictures is one of the most popular activities online. Take advantage of this trend by using photographs to promote your employment brand.
- Cool photo tools I cited were Bitstrips, Recite This and Animoto.
- I suggested an Instagram strategy for finding and communicating with passive candidates.
- I mentioned how Google shows love to video in its search results and mentioned Vine as well as my success with video when I was working at Microsoft.
- I also asked about your employer brand and mentioned a few ways to research it plus, I gave you a template for surveying your company.

What else? Umm... I think that's it. Of Course, you can always flip back a few pages and see if I missed anything. Did I miss anything?

:-)

BE PREPARED BEFORE YOU ENGAGE!

My next set of tips and strategies are centered around efficiency. Taking some time on the front end to prepare your interactions with candidates and hiring managers will pay off well in terms of time saved and reputation building. At least, that has been my experience.

SOURCING SERVICE LEVEL AGREEMENT

It can be said for any occupation that efficiency is everything, but I think it is especially relevant when you are retained to develop leads for a client. I cannot tell you how much time I have wasted over the years due to miscommunication between what a client wants verses what they say they want verses my giving them what they asked for originally. Eventually, I learned a simple but powerful truth that helped me to protect my sanity and maintain a solid client relationship. What's that? Simple. I added a Sourcing Service Level Agreement to my work process. Let me get a little deeper into what I mean.

WHAT IS A SOURCING SERVICE LEVEL AGREEMENT?

A Sourcing Service Level Agreement (SSLA) is an agreed upon set of deadlines between the sourcers and the recruiter being supported. It is intended to serve as a means to set end-user expectations and establishing a process that can be benchmarked and used for evaluating performance. To be effective, the SSLA must have penalty clauses associated with the failure to deliver on said agreement.

WHERE DOES THIS AGREEMENT BELONG IN THE RECRUITMENT PROCESS?

Whereas the process by which sourcers service their various clients may differ between organizations, here is a suggested method of implementation.

1. Recruiter makes a formal request for recruitment research from sourcer.
2. Sourcer replies by sending a SSLA to the recruiter requesting additional information.
3. Recruiter completes the SSLA and sends to sourcer, along with a job requisition (when possible) and tentative times/dates for an initial meeting to discuss the SSLA.
4. Recruiter and sourcer meet to discuss the SSLA. It is at the conclusion of this meeting that the engagement begins and work commences.
5. At the agreed upon date (as set in the SSLA), sourcer and recruiter meet to discuss and disposition each candidate submitted.

WHAT METRICS CAN BE GATHERED BASED ON THE SOURCING SERVICE LEVEL AGREEMENT?

The ultimate metric of any sourcing function is to ascertain how many of the leads referred resulted in actual hires made. However, as there are so many variables beyond the sourcer's control, it is recommended that additional landmarks be considered.

- How many of the leads that the sourcer supplied were accepted* by the Recruiter?
- How many of the leads that the sourcer supplied were interviewed?

- How many of the leads that the sourcer supplied were deferred to other opportunities within the company?
- How many of the leads that the sourcer supplied were refused because they did not match the recruiter's request?
- How many of the leads that the sourcer supplied were hired into the company?

*Accepted leads are to be interpreted as "the prospect that the sourcer supplied to the recruiter met the minimum requirements as detailed in the SSLA."

SOURCING SERVICE LEVEL AGREEMENT

This Sourcing Service Level Agreement (heretofore referred to as SSLA) serves as a formal agreement between the sourcing organization and the customer requesting recruitment research. The scope of the tasks that the sourcing organization can be expected to perform include, but are not limited to, the following work:

- RESUME MINING: The sourcing organization scours the internet to find the resumes of active job seekers who have their resumes posted online, and not necessarily submitted to job boards (ie: Monster.com).
- RESUME BLITZ: The sourcing organization works in concert with various recruiting teams to build a pipeline of prospects in a particular geographic area in advance of a pending job fair.

- COMPETITIVE RESPONSE: The sourcing organization seeks out active and passive job seekers of a certain company that has recently announced layoffs.
- PASSIVE LEAD GENERATION: The sourcing organization researches luminaries and their colleagues and pursues them for future opportunities.
- UPDATE CONTACT INFORMATION: The sourcing organization finds current contact information when a candidate's records are out of date.
- SOCIAL MEDIA RECRUITING: The sourcing organization works with the marketing department to develop and deliver a recruiting message across various social networks, blogs and online forums. After which, The sourcing organization will develop a warm lead list based on respondents to this campaign.

All requests must be submitted first to _____ of the sourcing organization. No request should be considered valid until it has been approved by _____ of the sourcing organization.

_____ of the sourcing organization is ultimately responsible for accepting and prioritizing the project requests. This is done to better serve you and to insure a reasonable timeline to complete the requested task. As such, some projects may be refused due to workload.

The sourcing organization is responsible for inputting the leads submitted into the Applicant Tracking System. Customer is responsible for feedback on each rejected lead supplied by The sourcing organization at the point of receipt.

PLEASE COMPLETE THE ENTIRE FORM BELOW

Job Title: _____

Requisition Number (if applicable)
_____

How long has the job been open?
_____

Is relocation an option? [ ] Yes   [ ] No

What have you done to fill this position so far?
_____

What are some of the challenges that you have encountered while trying to fill this role?
_____

What are the skills that the candidate must have in order to be considered for this opportunity?
_____

What are the skills that would be nice for a candidate to have, but are not mandatory?
_____

KEYWORD LIST

Please list as many keywords that you can that are relevant to your request. For example, alternative job titles, acronyms, competitors, conferences, products and the names of experts and luminaries associated with the industry.

- _____
- _____
- _____
- _____
- _____
- _____

SUPPORTING DOCUMENTS

When submitting the SSLA, please forward with it any documents that will support your request. Ideally, one or more of the following:

- A job description
- Example resumes to emulate (Candidates that were previously interviewed and/or hired into the role)

SCHEDULE OF EVENTS

- On (date) at (time) we will meet to discuss the SSLA.
- By the end of the business day on (date) The sourcing organization would have submitted X leads.
- On (date) at (time) we will meet to discuss the progress of this project and disposition every lead that has been accepted to date.
- On (date) at (time) will mark the final meeting concerning this project. At this time, a continuance may also be discussed and agreed upon.

###

CREATE STRATEGIC PARTNERSHIPS

Once you have an agreement with the hiring managers you are supporting, it would be wise to set up strategic partnerships inside your company. Here are a few worth considering.

- MARKETING - As you produce and distribute content that promotes your company culture, it will be useful to have a reservoir to pull from. More than likely the marketing department will have information that is "shareworthy."
- COMPANY EXPERTS - If you work for a tech company and you write or share articles on tech, it is to your advantage if people within your company comment on them as well. It will help in SEO and lend credibility to your company as well.
- COWORKER SUPPORTERS - Build up an army of co-workers that you can lean on to like, +1, share and comment on items you produce.

IF THIS THEN THAT

Walk into any skyscraper in the USA and somewhere in the corner is a fire extinguisher encased in glass that says, "In Case of Emergency" or, something along those lines. More often than not, there is also a map of the floor showing where the nearest exits are. My next suggestion for you is to create an engagement map addressing every possible scenario you are likely to encounter online.

For example, what do you do if someone inquires on your Facebook page about the status of their resume? What if someone keeps posting offensive comments on your Google Plus page? How do you react to a negative post about the company? How do you dispute a false claim against a specific recruiter working at your company?

Create a flowchart that addresses these and other points. If the idea of this is intimidating to you, I suggest a couple of options: 1) Contact an agency like Bernard Hodes Group [29] to create an engagement map customized to your needs or 2) base your engagement map on the social media policies of others. [30]

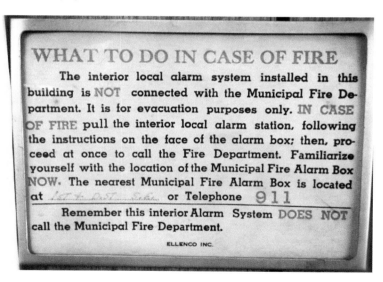

WHAT TO DO IN CASE OF FIRE

The interior local alarm system installed in this building is NOT connected with the Municipal Fire Department. It is for evacuation purposes only. IN CASE OF FIRE pull the interior local alarm station, following the instructions on the face of the alarm box; then, proceed at once to call the Fire Department. Familiarize yourself with the location of the Municipal Fire Alarm Box NOW. The nearest Municipal Fire Alarm Box is located at _____ or Telephone 911

Remember this interior Alarm System DOES NOT call the Municipal Fire Department.

ELLENCO INC.

PLOTTING SOCIAL DOMINATION

Once you have your internal processes in place, it will be time to start planning your outreach strategy.

[29] Bernard Hodes Group is an agency that specializes in recruitment marketing. It was acquired by Findly in 2012. [www.findly.com]
[30] The blog - "Social Media Governance" has a policy database of 240+ social media policies. [socialmediagovernance.com/policies.php]
[Above] Photo by Dave Hopton. Used here in compliance to a Creative

I would suggest you begin targeting groups frequented by the people you want to recruit, the influencers in those groups and thought leaders on the internet itself. The next set of tips will help you accomplish that.

LINKEDIN GROUPS

LinkedIn has a LOT of groups devoted to all sorts of professions and niche concerns. Not sure if you are aware of this, but each group on LinkedIn has demographic data on where its members are located, their industry focus and level of seniority. To access that data, click the information icon on the group homepage. At this writing, it is to the right of the yellow "Join" button. (See the arrow?)

Clicking the icon will bring you to a page similar to the one below. Judging by the stats on this group, if I

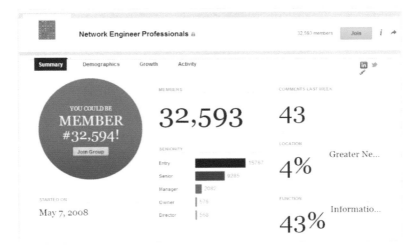

wanted to recruit Network Engineers operating at the entry level, this would be the place to be. I also would look at the links on the page like "Growth" to see how often this group takes on new members and "Activity" to see how active the group is. Information like this helps me determine which LinkedIn group is worth my time. (LinkedIn only allows you to join a maximum of 50 groups at once, so be choosy.)

FACEBOOK LISTS

Did you know that you could create a Facebook newsfeed focused on a certain interest? This function is called a "list" and it is very handy for monitoring industry news and tracking competitors. Let me show you how to set one up.

You begin by searching Facebook for whatever page interests you. For demo purposes, I am looking for the Facebook presence of the blog - TechCrunch.

Once I find the Facebook page I am looking for, I choose "Add to Interest Lists..." from the navigation bar. (See the arrow?)

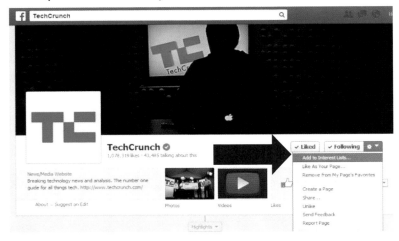

Another window appears and from that, I choose "New List" from the next window.

I am brought to a page called "Create New List" and TechCrunch is already selected, so I click the "Next" button. (Shown at the top of the next page.)

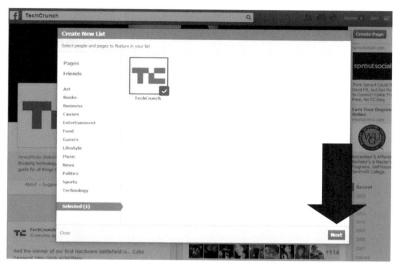

I call the list "Tech Stuff" and choose to make it private by selecting "Only Me." Afterward, I click the "Done" button.

When I return to my Facebook "Home" page, I see "Tech Stuff" in the left hand column. It is in the "Interests" section. Clicking on "Tech Stuff" I see only the updates from TechCrunch. How convenient is that?! Very.

TWITTER LISTS

There is a lot of data flowing on Twitter and it is very easy to become overwhelmed. Twitter lists can be a great way to keep up with a select crowd of people and / or organizations. Just like with the Facebook lists example, setting up a Twitter list lets you focus on the updates of certain people. Make sense?

Setting up a Twitter list is easy and adding names to the list you create is even easier. Let me show you how.

STEP ONE: Click on the "me" icon at the top of your Twitter home page. (Hmm… let's make this step one - B. Step One - A is to set up a Twitter account.)

STEP TWO: Select "Lists" in the box in the upper left hand corner.

STEP THREE: Select "Create list" and a new window will open. You can enter the name of your list, a description (optional) and make the list public or private (for your use only).

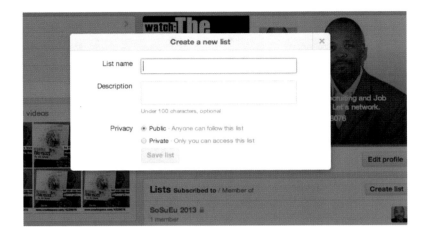

All the lists you create or subscribe to will be shown in this section of Twitter. (See my lists below?)

To add someone to your Twitter list, visit their profile and click the gear icon beneath their profile. Once you do, a drop down menu will appear. (As shown below.) Select "add or remove from lists" from the pull-down menu.

You can then add a person to a list **you** created by selecting the empty box next to the desired list. A checkmark will appear in the box. You're done.

I feel like we are nearing the homestretch and there is still much to say. Bear with me as I I think a moment on what I need to say next. Oh! Yeah, I remember now.

QUALITY > QUANTITY

As a recruiter, it is a constant temptation to send out a blanket email to multiple candidates with the hope that a significant percentage will reply. I want to suggest a different course of action. Mind you, it will be more time consuming! However, the pay off is much greater than playing the numbers game.

In a nutshell, I suggest that you go out of your way to personalize every approach you make to passive candidates. I want to share a few methods to accomplish that. The first is what I humbly refer to as "The Perfect Prospecting Letter."

Let's say I was looking for someone skilled in wireless network technology and happened along a comment in a LinkedIn group. Based on what I read, I suspect that the person might make a good hire. So, I send an inmail along these lines...

(1) SUBJECT: **I heard (Prospect's name) thinks 802.11x is a waste of time and money. Is that true?**

(Insert Prospect's Name Here):

(2) I read your comment in the LinkedIn group - Wireless Geeks. When you asked," Is 802.11x a waste of your time and money?" I thought to myself,

I hope not! (3) I just invested a lot of time and money hiring seven Certified Wireless Network Professionals (CWNA) for my employer. (4) When I read your comments on how you have leveraged this technology, I began wondering if it would be a good idea for you to chat with our CTO. (Seriously!) Time permitting, I would welcome the opportunity to discuss this possibility with you. (5) Are you available for a 6-minute chat? Please advise...

Obviously, you do not have to add numbers within your reply letter. They are there only as a reference for our example, so as to identify the purpose for each line.

(1) Make sure your email is short and sweet (4 lines ideally) with an attention grabbing subject line.

(2) I identify how I found them.

(3) I cite my qualifications as a recruiter VERY concisely.

(4) A bit of flattery and then I tease them on the benefit of speaking with me. Hopefully speaking to our CTO is appealing to them. (smile)

(5) Suggest a very short time to get better acquainted with the hope that the initial conversation will be so engrossing that it will lead to additional phonecalls and a hire. (smile)

FACEBOOK GRAPH SEARCH

I like Facebook for a variety reasons, but one of my favorite reasons is its graph search capabilities. Why? It helps me to send very personalized messages to prospects. Allow me to explain...

Let's imagine for a moment that you are looking to recruit software developers in the Atlanta area. You might do a search like the one pictured below.

Facebook does not give an exact number, but they do list the results as being over a hundred. (See the arrow pointing to it?) As Facebook has a billion users (more or less) that 100+ number could be substantial. So, I decide to refine my results by adding additional criteria.

In the right hand column is a section called "Likes

and Interests." In that section, I type in the phrase "Star Trek" because I am a fan of the franchise. (Smile)

Facebook returns nine results. So now, I have a list

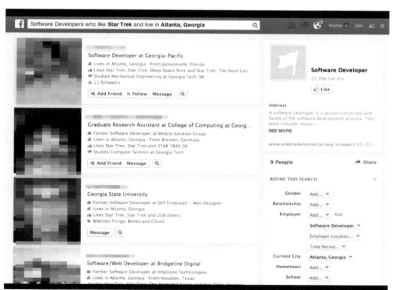

of nine software developers in Atlanta who like Star Trek. While I may be tempted to reach out to them via Facebook, I take note of their name and where they work and look them up on LinkedIn. Why? Some people are very guarded about their Facebook profile and do not relish the idea of recruiters viewing their Facebook data. I can dig it.

In the event that I am unsuccessful in finding them on LinkedIn, I would track down their work email address and attempt to connect with them that way. For example, among the results I found in my search for software developers, I noticed that someone worked for a company called - Smartbim. To get an idea of how they format their emails, I do the following search.

(email OR contact) "*@smartbim.com"

Just in case you did not read my last book - Resume Forensics (hint-hint), let me explain my search string. I am asking Google to look for the term "email" or the term "Contact" on a web page. I am also using the wildcard command (that's the asterix) to find any word or phrase that comes before "@smartbim.com." Check out one of the results!

Reed Construction Data and Source2 Announce Formation of ...
www.reedconstructiondata.com/.../reed-construction-data-and-source2-a... ▾
Oct 6, 2010 - (JavaScript must be enabled to view this email address), 678-756-5056 ...
SMARTBIM, LLC: Candice **Dobra, candice.dobra@smartbim.com**, ...

It would appear that based on this result, Smartbim's email format is firstname.lastname@smartbim.com. Now all I have to do is send some version of my prospecting letter with a mention (or two) of Star Trek to make it personal and the odds of that person replying to my email increases greatly. Make sense?

OTHER PERSONALIZATION RESOURCES

People tend to use the same username across various webpages. Case in point, I use "jimstroud" as my username on YouTube, LinkedIn, Twitter, Pinterest and just about every social network I am a member of. Chances are if you find someone of interest on one social network, they will be a member of at least one other social network.

Before reaching out to a passive candidate, see if they are active on one or more social networks. By doing so, you might get insight into their personal interests which will help you write a better prospecting letter. Make sense? A great resource for this type of research is Knowem [www.knowem.com].

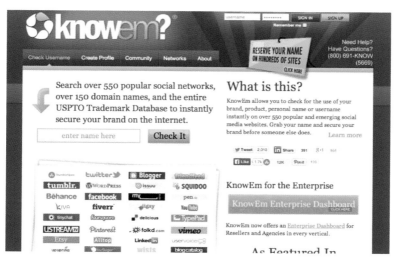

Knowem checks if a username is active on 550+ websites. I've used it often and recommend it.

Pipl [www.pipl.com] is the most comprehensive people search on the web. At least, according to their
own website. My experience with Pipl is that it is
scary good. Searching on a name, email, username
or phone will return results that you might miss on
other search engines.

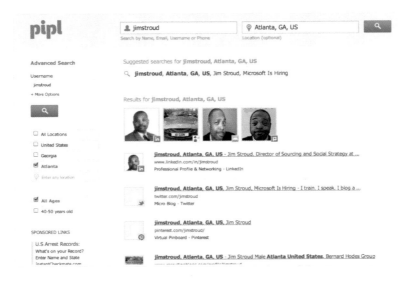

WHAT ABOUT THE PEOPLE YOU DO NOT HIRE?

What if you lured several people into your recruiting
web and for some reason or another, you do not hire
them. Maybe they were not interested in your
opportunity or perhaps, it was simply a matter of your
hiring someone else instead of them. In any regard,
there will be some candidates that you want to keep
track of and moreover, you want them to remain
interested in your company. Well, I have a few ideas
on how to do that very thing. (Insert dramatic music
here.)

- Use Watch That Page [www.watchthatpage.com] to monitor changes on the web. Say you find a resume on someone's blog. You speak to them and for whatever reason, you do not hire them. With WTP you monitor the URL of that resume and when they make a change to it, you are notified via email. This tool could very well help you contact someone at just the right time in order to renew their interest in your company. (wink)
- Poll the managers at your company and ask them what their biggest headaches are. Make a list and send it to candidates for their feedback. (Assuming that it does not reveal anything proprietary.) Ask them to develop a plan for resolving the issue and attach their resume as proof of their qualifications. Present the most compelling answers to management for special consideration.
- Treat candidates in your Applicant Tracking System like preferred customers. Give them exclusive content and advanced notice of company news and events prior to making them public. This is what I am thinking: a) invitations to Google Hangouts exclusive to them, b) advanced notice of careerfairs, c) MP3 conversations between recruiters and hiring managers discussing jobs they need filled and d) whitepapers and ebooks related to their professional interest.

Umm... Okay, that's all I got. At least, on this subject, for now. I do plan on writing a third book related to sourcing and/or recruiting but, not sure what that will be. Connect with me online and stay in touch. When I know, I will let you know. Okay? Turn the page for one last recommended resource. Later...

Sourcing is cool.

Proof

Made in the USA
Charleston, SC
28 February 2014